Clif,

Bob and I are delighted you have entered our lives. We look forward to a continuing friendship.

Blessings,
Marcia Shepherd

Shake the Dust — and Move on

by
Marcia Shepherd

authorHOUSE®

AuthorHouse™
1663 Liberty Drive, Suite 200
Bloomington, IN 47403
www.authorhouse.com
Phone: 1-800-839-8640

First published by AuthorHouse   10/15/2007

ISBN: 978-1-4343-3549-4 (sc)

Library of Congress Control Number: 2007907480

Printed in the United States of America
Bloomington, Indiana

This book is printed on acid-free paper.

Dedication

to

my husband,

Bob,

the answer to my prayers in 1972,
the fulfillment of my dreams
ever since

Contents

Preface

When I started this book, I thought it was all about me. I have since come to see that it has little to do with me. The book started with the nucleus of a disappointing situation and a powerful phrase, *Shake the dust and move on*, that propelled me through it. Over the last five years, this concept has evolved and become more meaningful as I have worked my way through other rough spots in life. It is my hope that this book will inspire, encourage, and bless you as you use it to reflect upon your own life.

This book could be a meaningful personal study. However, it is especially designed (with applications and discussion questions) to be used in small group study. The dynamics of a small group study can be powerful. I learned in my studies as a counselor that much healing can take place when people are in a safe, confidential, non-threatening environment where others listen without judging and provide each person an opportunity to examine his/her own thoughts. My pastor, Stuart Hodges, of Waters Edge Church is a strong advocate of small group study. He feels that small groups are where real "body" work takes place as people examine their lives in the context of biblical principles. This is where relationships form a solid base for spiritual, intellectual, and emotional growth and fulfillment.

I hope that this book will fuel many positive relationships and nurture hungry hearts with questions that lead each person to disclose his own experience and connect with the experience of others. As we each open our lives to become more transparent with each other, we soon discover that what seems to apply only to "me," is often universal. So, it's not really about me after all. That in itself is comforting and encouraging. Be blessed as you examine your own life and as you determine to *shake the dust and move on.*

Acknowledgements

I want to thank my daughter and her husband, Sarah and Scott Burggraf; my husband, Bob Shepherd; and our sons--Rob, and Jon Shepherd for personal experiences they graciously allowed me to share. I thank Bob and the teachers in our family: Nicole Shepherd, Monica Shepherd, and Sarah Burggraf for their proofreading skills. I thank Jon Shepherd for his artistic advice and creative castle illustration. I thank Bob, Rob, and Sarah for their analytical skills in helping me cut the fat and stay focused. I am grateful to have such a multi-talented, creative team. I also thank Jim and Ethel Shepherd and Tim and Susan Smith for experiences they allowed me to share.

In addition, I acknowledge Susie Engle-Hill for her encouragement and help in reviewing much of the book. Finally, I want to thank my colleagues: Michele Ross for reading and responding to the manuscript, and Vickie Herzog, and Randall Stowe, for helping me through the technological challenges.

I

Sever Roots of Discord

Perseverance is a positive, powerful characteristic that propels people through the darkness of grief, pain, setback, rejection, and opposition. Perseverance pays rich dividends and accounts for great achievements. Giving up, stopping short of a goal, or making an excuse to quit runs counter to most motivational "never-give-up" messages programmed into the conscience of successful people.

However, there are some situations that do not fit the typical, motivational model for success. There are some reasons that validate taking another course of action. There are some circumstances that demand an alternate plan. In short, there are times to prudently, decisively, without a twinge of guilt, *Shake the dust and move on.*

One of the most basic examples of this principle came to me through my friend, Susan, who has been married nearly thirty years. She and her husband, Tim, raised two sons who are now married and headed toward successful, productive lives. When her sons were ready to leave the family home, Susan expressed a fundamental concept that is refreshingly honest and liberating:

> You are twenty-one and ready to move on. Your dad and I had never raised kids before you. We made some mistakes, and we did some things that were right. Accept that we tried our best. Don't get stuck on the past. Don't live your life blaming us for your shortcomings.
>
> Get over it! Move on!

From what I know of their lives, Susan and Tim are good parents. They offered their sons numerous advantages and created many positive bonds. Yet, whether a person is raised in a harmonious environment or in a dysfunctional mess, Susan's advice is a positive affirmation of an energizing principle: "Leave the dirt behind." Inherent in her words is the admonition to not let hurts from the past dominate the future.

Oprah Winfrey is an admirable example of a person who suffered immense misery and abuse as a child.

Even though Oprah is a high profile target for the media, she publicly confessed her past—defusing what might have generated some ugly publicity. Oprah obviously determined not to let the pain from her past dictate the direction of her future. She acknowledges her abuse but has shaken the dust of discord and dysfunction and moved on to a healthy, successful life.

I, too, have found that much of my success in marriage and in life has come from severing some negative roots of the past. Negative, dysfunctional relationships in marriage and parenting frequently lead to similar, repetitive behavior in the next generation.

I grew up in a family where my mom and dad were at odds, and divorce was frequently threatened. I felt loved and was given all the material comforts money could buy, but our family was a wreck. Mom seemed to hate Dad and his whole family. There were frequent blow-ups and even overnight separations. It was not uncommon for Mom to impulsively rush me into the car and drive us to her mother's to spend the night. Dad would always come through with compromises, promises, and the best peace-making skills he had to re-unite our family. One family upheaval occurred minutes before my first big event of high school --a spring concert. I had a new yellow chiffon dress with matching yellow heels. My choral group had practiced for weeks, preparing for this public event. A few hours before the event, my parents were engaged in a fierce verbal battle. I made arrangements to go to the concert with a friend. I remember walking on stage and carefully finding my place on the risers. I had a smile on my face, but a lump in my throat—not knowing if the current battle between my parents would be resolved or end their marriage. I hardly remember a family vacation, a major holiday, or a special event in my life that was not painfully infused with emotional turmoil between my parents.

After witnessing such marital conflict, I was not eager to rush into marriage myself. However, as a young person, I had already taken a major step in severing negative family roots by becoming a committed Christian and an active member of the church. Fortunately, my best friend, Louise, was part of a church-going family who always had room for one more—me. From age twelve, I regularly attended church with this family until I was old enough to drive myself.

Still, it was only after graduating from college and entering my profession as a teacher that I began to seriously contemplate marriage. Determined to avoid my parents' pitfalls, I earnestly sought the Lord's direction for a husband. I prayed for a husband—a man like David.

I knew the Old Testament character, David, was not perfect, but he was called "a man after God's own heart" (I Sam. 13:14). To me, David represents the calm, gentle nature of a *shepherd*, the strength of a *soldier*, and the sensitivity of a *poet/musician*. That's what I wanted in a husband.

Two years passed. At age twenty-four, I felt time was passing me by. I started graduate school, seeking a husband as much as a degree. As I prayed for a husband, I began knitting a man's vest. I called it a "faith vest" and trusted the Lord to supply the man for the vest. Seven days after completion of the vest, I met the man! His name wasn't David, but he was a *shepherd*—Robert Shepherd. He was a teacher currently pursuing a commission in the U.S. Army—*a soldier.* He also sang in church—*a musician.*

Was it love at first sight? No. There was, however, a mutual admiration, openness and honesty that quickly generated into a loving friendship and a romance based on Christian commitment, with mutual values, interests and ideals. Our proposal, engagement and marriage took place within nine months of our first meeting. The faith vest I had knit was too snug! The Lord had provided (abundantly above) all I had asked and more.

Our marriage has stood the test of 35 years and three wonderful children who are each married with harmonious homes of their own. We are by no means perfect, but in following God's plan instead of my hereditary family model, I severed specific roots of discord for myself, our children, and their children. I will forever be grateful for the education, material blessings, and love shown to me by various members of my childhood family, but where there were dysfunctional patterns, I have determined, with God's grace, to shake the dust and move on.

APPLICATION: What roots of discord do you need to sever?

_____

_____

_____

_____

_____

_____

_____

_____

_____

_____

_____

_____

Pray for God's wisdom, strength,
and guidance to help you.

Chapter I: Sever Roots of Discord

Pause and Ponder:

A good marriage is based not only on finding the right person but on *becoming* the right person.

Word Power:

"And I pray that you being rooted and established in love, may have power together with all the saints, to grasp how wide and long and high and deep is the love of Christ…"

(Ephesians 3:17b-18).

Body Builders for reflection and discussion:

1. What are the hereditary strengths and weaknesses you have inherited from your family, physically? emotionally? spiritually?

2. What personal characteristics foster a good marriage?

3. If married, what qualities most attracted you to your spouse?

   If single, what qualities are you seeking in a spouse? Or what are ways people can be most helpful in relating to you as a single person?

4. Which parenting techniques from your own upbringing would you like to continue?

   Which parenting techniques from your own upbringing would you like to change?

5. Why is it important (to you and to your children) that you forgive and let go of mistakes and hurts from the past?

II

Embrace Enduring Change

Most of us understand that life is too brief to waste time, energy, talent, and resources where even the most exhaustive effort will not be received. However, many of us are natural *fixers* and like to zoom in like a super hero determined to save the day. Unfortunately, in the great Metropolis of life, some people do not welcome help. That does not negate the fact that such people may desperately need help. It just means (for whatever reason) they are not ready or cannot receive help that is offered. This is one of those times to **shake the dust and move on.** Otherwise, it is possible to become an enabler for negative, destructive behavior and fall prey to needy, manipulative individuals who demand time and deplete resources but never change. It is like the adage: "Give a hungry man a fish and tomorrow he will still be hungry.

Teach a hungry man how to fish, and he will never be hungry again." Huge difference!

Three Gospels: Matthew, Mark, and Luke record a specific assignment Jesus gave his disciples. First, Jesus equipped the disciples with supernatural gifts to heal the sick, raise the dead, cleanse lepers, and drive out demons. He then sent the disciples to share these wondrous gifts, free—without charge. "Freely ye have received, freely give" (Matthew 10:8). How could anyone reject such gifts? Why would anyone refuse such Divine help? Yet, Jesus concludes his assignment with, "Whoever will not receive, accept, and welcome you nor listen to your message as you leave that house or town, shake the dust of it from your feet." What would cause people to refuse help or reject blessings? Perhaps, their paradigm is too small. Maybe it is fear of the unknown. Change is often unwelcome. Jesus does not explain. He simply uses the imperative command, "Take your blessing with you and shake the dust from your feet" (Matt.10:13-15). Jesus demonstrates this principle as He frequently slips away from Pharisees who use manipulative words and destructive entrapments (John 10:31, 39, 11:54).

A modern day example is well made when our daughter, Sarah, went on a mission trip to minister to homeless people on the streets of New York City. Each team was trained and equipped with supplies by New

York School of Urban Ministries (NYSUM). Members of the teams were given blankets, toiletries, food, and Bibles to hand out as they shared an encouraging message of hope and salvation. I remember the advice given to the team by one of the leaders:

> Look into the eyes of the people. Look for those who will receive your help. Some may want to rush up and seize your possessions. Do not let them! What you have can be easily sold for drugs or alcohol around the corner. Look for those whom you can help. Give to those who will receive, but do not let your gifts be taken from you.

Another example of enablement rather than empowerment may be found in the work place. Our youngest son, Jonathan, has an exceptional work ethic. When he sees a job that needs to be done, he does it. Jon is one to seize the moment and tackle the task. He is currently working for our city sanitation department. The work he does requires maximum strength, effort, and endurance. Jon's work is rigorous but it recognizes his efforts with benefits, schooling, new opportunities, and promotions.

This job is a major contrast to a job Jon held during and following his high school years. He worked just as diligently detailing vehicles for a car dealership. Unfortunately, there was no one in leadership or no system in place to recognize his efforts or protect him from "slackers" who let work pile up on their shifts to be dumped on Jon.

Jon worked at the dealership for over five years. The more earnestly he worked, the more work there was for him to do. Jon was young and loyal. He gave it his best effort. The work place took, but it gave little in return. People sometimes stay in jobs like this for security, loyalty, or simply fear of change. Life is too short! Seek enduring change, not enablement for a negative situation. Hard work can be energizing when the environment is right. It can be draining when people "take" rather than "receive" what is offered. Valuable lessons can be learned even from negative situations. However, it is often better to shake the dust and move on than to enable a negative situation.

Not all enabling situations are external. Sometimes people enable attitudes such as jealousy, anger, selfishness, guilt, etc. to take up residence *within* their lives. Sometimes, people who have trouble receiving help are enjoying the pleasure of their pain. That seems like an oxymoron, but most of us can identify with situations in which we have held tightly to self-righteous justifications for attitudes we know are wrong. It is possible to enable the guilt of a mistake or a sin to dominate one's life. In such cases, people may assume the role of a martyr and reason that they deserve to be punished. They may claim their sin is too big to be forgiven. How arrogant! How egotistical to think that any sin is bigger than God's grace or outside the boundaries of His forgiveness. It is not God's grace that is lacking; it is human reluctance to surrender, to repent, and to receive His grace that keeps people separated from God. Such actions are essential to shaking the dust and moving on.

Some people even find creative ways to use their guilt-ridden past to help others from making the same mistakes. For example, a person I know of who had an abortion, later became an advocate for adoption and adopted children of her own.

APPLICATION: What action do you need to take to foster enduring change versus enablement?

_____

_____

_____

_____

_____

_____

_____

_____

_____

_____

_____

Ask God to forgive, heal, and help you
to make that change.

Chapter II: Embrace Enduring Change

Pause and Ponder:

How do you respond to a beggar asking for money? Does your response foster change or enablement?

Word Power:

Peter's response to a crippled beggar: "Silver or gold I do not have, but what I have I give you. In the name of Jesus Christ of Nazareth, walk" (Acts 3:6).

Consider the parable of the Good Samaritan (Luke 10:30-35).

Body Builders for Reflection and Discussion

1. Consider times you have offered something to a person who did not receive what you gave (a compliment, advice, help, or a gift).

2. Consider and share times when others have taken advantage of you? your efforts? your resources? How might you have prevented this situation?

3. Do you have difficulty receiving from others? How do you respond to a compliment? encouragement? generosity?

4. What attitudes or emotions are you enabling to control areas of your life?

5. Ask God to help you seek positive, enduring changes.

III

Emerge into New Beginnings

Remember what it was like to graduate from high school? There were all these emotions swirling within your head. It was sad to leave what was familiar, but at the same time there was an excitement because a new journey was about to begin. Some endings generate intense sorrow. Yet, underneath all the debris of a dead end, somewhere deep within the soil of sadness, roots are already forming, and a new beginning is about to emerge. As scripture declares, "Joy comes in the morning" (Ps.30:5). For the child of God, as cliché as it may sound, "All things work together for good…" (Rom.8:28).

Sad endings can become beautiful beginnings at any age. Our son, Rob, loves basketball. He started playing in community leagues in third grade. His talent did not always match his enthusiasm, but he loved to play basketball and idealized a future in professional leagues.

Rob was in seventh grade when we moved from Kansas to Virginia. He enrolled in a Christian school with a competitive basketball program starting with a JJV team in sixth grade and continuing with junior varsity and varsity teams into high school. Rob admired the blue, white, and gold uniforms of the team. Next year, as an eighth grader, he would have his chance to try out.

Tryouts were announced at the beginning of the new school year. Rob's excitement soared as fellow classmates encouraged him to sign up. The eighth graders selected would likely play on the junior varsity team the following year. So much was at stake. The day for tryouts came. The eighth grade team was chosen. The cuts were made.

My husband found Rob sitting on the steps outside the gym, tears rolling down his warm flushed cheeks. Cuts were final. A door was slammed! Thoughts of that moment can still produce a lump in my throat. Other parents mentioned how well Rob had played and what an encourager he was to others on the team. It didn't matter. It didn't lessen the pain or change the circumstances.

Francis, one of the team member's mothers, consoled Rob and *insisted* that he try out for one of the basketball teams at her church. As it turned out, the large Baptist church Francis attended had numerous basketball teams and offered a lot of additional activities. Rob played basketball on the church's teams for the next five years. He later served as an assistant coach and eventually coached his own team. Our whole family became active in that church. Rob later became an intern in the youth ministry of that church. He accepted a call to ministry there, was ordained as a minister of the Gospel, graduated from Southwest Baptist Theological Seminary, and had connections from that same church that have led to Waters Edge Church where he ministers today. Shaking the dust of a lost opportunity, led Rob to a new beginning.

Much like Rob's cut from the team tryouts, businesses and organizations can sometimes be ruthless. Cutbacks, downsizing, and even buyouts can result in closed doors. Being squeezed out of an organization or company in which much energy, talent, and time have been invested can be painful. It hurts. It's unfair. It's wrong. Yet, it happens. It happens even to the very best, most intelligent, gifted, faithful employees who have done nothing to deserve the cut.

Arbitrary cuts are sometimes based on pure economics or organizational needs. Sometimes, such changes occur because of advances in technology. The list of reasons goes on, and the reasons may seem logical and sound or they may be the result of someone's zeal, or manipulation. Whether the reasons are just or unjust, right or wrong, the impact at the moment is painful.

Like Rob not making the school team, such moments are crushing. I would love to be like Francis, the mother who insisted that Rob try out for another team. I would like to remind anyone who has been cut that there are other teams, other businesses, other organizations, and other opportunities. It's only a position that has been cut. It may have been a position that included benefits (salary, retirement, and other compensations). Yes, and it is unpleasant, unfortunate, and painful, but it is not the end; it is a transition toward a new beginning.

People who lose a position leave a little wiser. They take experience, training, and connections. They leave with the same skills and abilities that brought previous success. Those qualities can bring success again. It may take some time, but it is not a time to fret over the past. It's a time to harness the energy, talents, skills, and experience for a new team. It's time to consider new possibilities and break free to a new beginning.

Sometimes it is helpful to remember that many famous people have suffered setbacks and defeats. Jennifer Hudson, insulted by Simon and voted off of *American Idol*, went on to star in *Dream Girls* and win an Oscar. Theodor Geisel (Dr. Seuss) was turned down by several publishers before his success. Walt Disney's first cartoon company went bankrupt. Michael Jordan says, "I've missed more than 9000 shots in my career. I've lost almost 300 games. 26 times, I've been trusted to take the game winning shot and missed. I've failed over and over and over again in my life. And that is why I succeed."

These examples inspire us to remember that an ending is never the end. It is simply an occasion to emerge into a new beginning. Such an occasion occurred recently when a colleague of mine retired after more than thirty years in the same institution. Her retirement was like a graduation. It was a joyful celebration with a twinge of sadness. The poem, "Sand Castle Blueprint," was written for her farewell but serves as an appropriate addendum to this chapter.

Sand Castle Blueprint

Remember when you were a toddler,
Building sand castles on the beach?

At first, they were simple structures.
Yet beautiful,
because you shaped them with tiny hands
and a big imagination.

The tide came in, as it always does,
and washed away your primitive structure.
But your imagination grew, and the next sand castle
was bigger and better than the last.

Time passed; you used paper cups to mold towers,
and drew doors and windows
with a piece of broken seashell.

Lovely were the sand castles of childhood
Lovelier the sand castles of youth.
But today's sand castle is beyond compare.

Today, you formed a moat for your sand castle.
You added a drawbridge made of glass.

Today's castle combines former blueprints
with playful embellishments of the present.
Nothing is lost as the tide comes in.

Your blueprint expands; your imagination soars;
The best designs are yet to come.
Cherish the moment,
creating new sand castles on the beach.

Marcia Shepherd (2-2-07)

APPLICATION: Recall an experience in your life in which you failed to achieve a goal:

_____

_____

_____

_____

_____

_____

_____

_____

_____

_____

_____

_____

_____

Count your blessings and thank God that what appears to be the end, in His hands, is a new beginning.

Chapter III: Emerge into New Beginnings

Pause and Ponder:

Life can be very abrasive. Attitude is the factor that determines whether the roughest situations in life will grind a person down and dull his senses or polish his potential and sharpen his skills.

Word Power:

"He who goes out weeping, carrying seed to sow, will return with songs of joy, carrying sheaves with him" (Psalms 126:6).

Body Builders for Reflection and Discussion:

1. How has a defeat, disappointment, or ending emerged into a new direction or destination for you?

2. How have experiences (defeats or victories) caused you to grow and become a stronger, better person?

3. If your job or essential duties ended tomorrow, what "seeds" would you carry with you for a new start in life?

4. When an infant leaves the comfort of the womb, it is a painful journey into a new world. How

is this like leaving comfort zones in life? How is it like leaving one's past and becoming a Christian?

IV

Circumvent Circumstances

Despite tragic, irreversible circumstances, there are many heroic models in life who have triumphed over tragedy. As Robert H. Schuller claims in his book by the same title, these are people who serve as reminders to *Turn Your Scars into Stars*. These are people who do not give up on their dreams when the going gets rough. These are people without hands who, like Tony Melendez, learn to play the guitar with their toes. These are people like Joni Ericson Tada, paralyzed from the neck down, who paint gorgeous pictures with pencil/brush held between her teeth. Other examples might include Bethany Hamilton, a young teenage competitive surfer who continues surfing after the loss of her left arm from a shark attack. A dynamic person, Nick Vujicic, was born without arms or legs. Nick's website <Lifewithoutlimbs.org> is an inspiration. Nick sums up his life with the phrase, "Life without limbs to life without limits."

Among this host of gallant heroes who have shaken the dust and moved on is one of the most inspiring, humorous, delightful people I have ever met, Dan Miller. Dan was a young man with big dreams. He was captain and an all-star player of his high school league championship basketball team. Dan was competitive in football, baseball, and track. Some of his goals were to become a physical education teacher, get married, have children, and fly an airplane. Five weeks after high school graduation, Dan became ill with a debilitating, life threatening disease--polio. Ironically, Dan contracted the disease in 1955, just weeks before the Salk vaccine reached his small town of Pateros, Washington. Dan tells his incredible story in *Living, Laughing and Loving Life*. Visit Dan's website <<u>www.danmillerspeaker.</u> <u>com</u>> to learn how he has circumvented circumstances to achieve his dreams of flying a plane, becoming a P.E. teacher, and much more.

Other examples of circumventing circumstances include Thomas Edison whose many unsuccessful experiments led him to eventually create the first light bulb. The Wright brothers many failed attempts led them closer to overcoming the force of gravity and taking flight. Henry Ford, the founder of Ford Motor

Company, had numerous setbacks before his success. Ford concludes, "When everything seems to be going against you, remember that the airplane takes off against the wind, not with it."

Each person mentioned in this chapter has a memorable message. Each is a model for taking life's misfortunes and masterfully crafting them into powerfully positive new paths of achievement. Each of these individuals might have settled into the emotions of despondency, and defeat. No one could criticize them if they had camped out permanently in the Slough of Despair, but they didn't. The average person can learn much from these super hero mortals who often with humor, gratitude, and gallantry shook the dust of defeat and adversity and moved on.

Such fortitude can be found in other areas of life. My sister-in-law's brother, Benny, was greatly distressed over an unalterable state legislated decision to build a highway through his property. Benny, at first, protested the decision. Then, when it seemed there was no further recourse, he accepted plans for the inevitable, obtrusive highway to run through his property and destroy much of his farmland.

With revenue from the forced sale of his property, Benny decided to build a grocery shopette with gas pumps and located it on the edge of the new highway.

His country convenience store was in an ideal location between two small Missouri Ozark towns on Highway 60. Instead of wallowing in self-pity, Benny shook the dust, and moved on to greater financial success and satisfaction than he could have ever dreamed.

My husband's older brother, Jim, and his wife, Ethel, are an amazing couple who have endured immense tragedy. Their grandson, Daniel, was six when he leapt from a backyard swing set and landed with one leg under a riding lawn mower that his grandmother, Ethel, was driving. Ethel clamped both hands around the child's mangled leg to save his life from the loss of blood. She held on tightly until the 911 team arrived. Daniel survived the accident but, a few days later, lost his leg.

A few years after Daniel's accident, Jim and Ethel lost their only child, Louise, in a fatal car accident that killed both her and her son, Daniel. The tragedy led to an unpleasant court battle which resulted in Jim and Ethel gaining custody of their grand-daughter, Stacy, who was eleven at the time of the accident.

One of the age old questions in life is why do such tragedies occur, and why do they happen to good people? The fact is we live in a sinful, imperfect, fallen world, and it is only in the Kingdom of God that such matters can be put into perspective. However, people like Jim and Ethel give us a glimpse of heaven's glory. Their losses cannot be minimized, but they have risen above the ashes of grief and sorrow to continue on as kind, generous, loving people of faith. They raised their grand-daughter, became caretakers of Ethel's aging brother until his death, and recently celebrated their 50th wedding anniversary. Their enduring marriage is an example of reverence and love between two people who have grown better, not bitter.

A person may have no control over circumstances but can always choose how to react to those circumstances. As Michael Jordan once said, "Obstacles don't have to stop you. If you run into a wall, don't turn around and give up. Figure out how to climb it, go through it, or work around it." The important thing is to shake the dust, and start moving.

APPLICATION: What would you most like to do in life if you knew there was absolutely nothing holding you back?

_____

_____

_____

_____

_____

_____

_____

_____

_____

_____

_____

_____

Ask God to mold your dream to fit you personally and focus you in the right direction to make it a reality.

Chapter IV: Circumvent Circumstances

Pause and Ponder:

Instead of following well-worn paths formed by others, consider blazing a trail for others to follow.

Word Power:

"I can do everything through him who gives me strength" (Philippians 4:13).

Body Builders for Reflection and Discussion:

1. What unalterable circumstances have you faced? How have such circumstances affected you?

2. How do you explain tragedy to a person who blames God for it?

3. What makes heaven different from life on earth?

4. Who do you know who has circumvented circumstances, making the best of an unfortunate situation?

5. What are some of the strengths that people often gain from adversity?

V

Discover the Positive Side of "No"

When Nancy Reagan was First Lady, she promoted a drug-free society with the slogan, "Just say, No." This sounds easy enough, but people often need some coaching, some training, some positive examples to boldly say, "No," even to negative things like drugs.

I remember my years as a stay-at-home mom with three toddlers. Stay-at-home moms were becoming less common in the 1980s, so when organizations, neighbors, church, or school needed a volunteer, I was high on their contact list. It wasn't my expertise as much as my assumed availability that gave rise to numerous calls for volunteer service. I soon learned that if I was willing to put aside career plans to fulfill my goal of staying at home to raise our children, I was going to have to learn to politely, powerfully say, "No." For some, this may seem easy, but for many of us, the natural instinct is to say, "Yes," at the moment and regret the decision later.

I found the key to my success in effectively saying, "No" was to give myself some time. I stopped giving an immediate decision and learned to reply, "Let me think about it" or "I'll check our family calendar and let you know later." This tactic gave me time to process whether the request was something I needed or wanted to do versus something I felt pressured to do. Many times, I was better off turning down routine involvements that meant finding childcare and obligating myself to things that were not relevant to my own goal of caring for our children.

Those years of putting family first and learning to say, "No," have provided valuable tools for life. Today, I continue to analyze situations similarly. When asked to take on additional duties, I often ask if I may have time to think about it. I like to consider the possible impact of the request. This is not lack of dedication or commitment but a concentration on what is really important. It is a matter of safe-guarding my productiveness rather than diluting my efforts in too many directions to be most effective.

For those naturally amenable people pleasers who are prone to become over committed by taking on others' expectations, it may be time to shake the dust of unnecessary obligations, to overcome self-imposed guilt, and learn the positive aspects of saying, "No." Jesus is a striking example of one who often pulled away from the crowds and their demands. He sought rest from the tasks at hand, and He didn't always stop what he was doing to fulfill another's perceived need. Even when Jesus received word from His friends that Lazarus was dying, he did not come quickly as requested (John 11:5). Jesus is an example of one who did what was important versus what seemed urgent. The tyranny of the urgent doesn't have to rule our lives.

A benefit of learning to say, "No," is that I can be freer, less scheduled, and more productive. The additional benefit is that I may be getting out of the way for the selection of a person who may be eager to do what I turned down.

Saying "No" can sometimes be risky. Sylvester Stallone risked saying, "No" when he tried to market a script he had written called, **Rocky.** At a time when Stallone needed the sale, producers offered to buy the script, but would not use Stallone as the actor in the starring role. Stallone held out until he could both sell the script and star as Rocky (West). The rest is history. Discover the many positive benefits of just saying, "No."

APPLICATION: What area(s) in life could you improve by saying, "No"?

_____

_____

_____

_____

_____

_____

_____

_____

_____

_____

_____

_____

_____

Ask God to help you discern when and how to say
"No" and give you courage to follow through.

Chapter V: Discover the Positive Side of "No"

Pause and Ponder:

A person can disagree without being disagreeable.

Word Power:

"Get rid of all bitterness, rage, and anger, brawling and slander, along with every form of malice. Be kind and compassionate to one another, forgiving each other, just as in Christ God forgave you" (Ephesians 4:31-32).

Body Builders for Reflection and Discussion:

1. Recall a time in which you said "Yes" to something or to someone but should have said, "No".

2. What are some examples in which people have difficulty saying, "No?"

   (How about self gratifications such as eating too much, or not living a healthy lifestyle?)

3. How can pleasing people be in conflict with pleasing God?

4. Why is it that some parents have difficulty saying, "No," to their children?

5. Imagine a friend of yours has become a salesperson for a product you do not want.

   How do you tell your friend "No" without being unkind?

VI

Flee From Destruction

In September 2003, the weather report predicted Hurricane Isabel, a category five hurricane, was headed toward the East Coast and would likely make its way on land. As the hurricane blasted its way through North Carolina and headed toward our home in Hampton, Virginia, schools and businesses announced closings for the rest of the week. There was a raid on basic supplies and residents prepared to take shelter. My husband and I decided this would be a good time to visit our daughter in Ohio.

We recognized that this hurricane was a destructive, uncontrollable force. We knew that remaining in its path would not change its course, diminish its power, or protect what we valued. So, we heeded the warning and moved out of its way.

Like the hurricane, there is a personality disorder that is nearly as destructive and unalterable as this unpredictable storm. I am not referring to an irregular, difficult, or even cantankerous person. I am referring to the personality disorder known as *sociopath*.

There are subtle distinctions and differences among the labels sometimes used interchangeably as *sociopath, psychopath, and anti-social personality disorder* (APD).

However, each is used to characterize a person whose moral compass or conscience is weak, marred, or seemingly nonexistent.

On the surface, a sociopath can appear quite normal, even intelligent and charming. They are unlikely to seek help on their own because they do not believe they are at fault or need help. They are egotistical individuals who feel they can talk their way out of anything and outsmart people around them. Every week, the news covers reports of ordinary, everyday people just like you and me who have been taken advantage of or been destroyed by individuals who are probably sociopaths. Scott Peterson, a sociopath, was in the news for months (2004) while on trial for killing his pregnant wife and their unborn child. The thing to remember is such people lead relatively ordinary lives and appear quite normal. Sociopaths do not always become violent and frequently go unidentified unless they break the law and come under involuntary scrutiny. Sociopaths are family members, neighbors, and friends. They may be in the workplace, the community, and even the church.

The point here is that there are sometimes people in our circles of influence who appear somewhat normal but are not. They storm through life creating a great deal of turmoil for others. Can God change such a person? Of course. However, a person who is a sociopath does not usually *want* to be changed or even think he/she needs to be changed. If such a person is a relative or close acquaintance, it may be best to honor him/her as best you can, but shake the dust and move on.

While the sociopath is a dramatic example of a destructive personality, there are other destructive tendencies. Any addiction: alcohol, drugs, pornography, gambling, or even excessive shopping can destroy the life of the addict and negatively impact those around him. It is important to support and seek help for those who will receive it. It is also important to understand that help does not mean enabling such individuals to continue their destructive lifestyle. It is not a matter of giving up on a person. It doesn't mean we stop loving, or praying for a person who is destructive, but it may mean we leave the work of transformation to God while we shake the dust and move on.

David (Old Testament) is a powerful example of honoring the position of a person, King Saul, while shaking the dust and moving on. "While David was playing the harp, Saul tried to pin him to the wall with his spear, but David eluded him as Saul drove the spear into the wall. That night David made good his escape" (I Samuel 19:9b-10). As crazy and demented as Saul was, David still honored Saul's position as his king.

Saul was jealous of David's popularity and success. He formed many plots to capture and kill David. Yet, when David had the opportunity to harm Saul, he did not. Saul happened into a cave where David and some of his men were hidden farther back in the depths of the cave. David's soldiers knew that they could easily destroy Saul. Instead, David slipped up unnoticed and cut off a corner of Saul's robe. Later, David even repented of this action:

Afterward David was conscience stricken for having cut off a corner of his robe. He said to his men, 'The Lord forbid that I should do such a thing to my master, the Lord's anointed, or to lift my hand against him; for he is the anointed of the Lord.' With these words David rebuked his men and did not allow them to attack Saul. And Saul left the cave and went his way (I Samuel 24:5-7).

David is an example of loyalty and restraint, even though he fled for his life. Consequently, David's moral integrity seemed to change Saul's attitude: Saul asked, "Is that your voice, David my son?" And he wept aloud. "You are more righteous than I," he said. "You have treated me well, but I have treated you badly" (I Samuel 24:16-17). This change in Saul must have been a welcome relief to David, but it is interesting to note that David never returned with Saul. Forgiveness does not mean giving the person another chance to be destructive. It does mean doing the right thing and freeing *yourself* of unnecessary bondage such as guilt, revenge, and lack of forgiveness.

Moving on in situations like David's can be a challenge. As Christians, we are commissioned to love unconditionally. We are directed to forgive "seventy times seven". Like David, we should be bound by the law of kindness and restraint. However, we are not God. We cannot change another person.

Unfortunately, people sometimes enter relationships *thinking* they can change another person. Our first child, Sarah, chose a husband whom her father and I felt from the beginning was not right for her. I had prayed for Sarah's husband since she was a baby and had looked forward to the time when she would wed. It was painful to see our intelligent child, who had a history of making wise choices, make what seemed to be such an enormous mistake. The emotion of love often overrides common sense and good judgment. It was evident that our strong-willed, independent daughter was going to follow her heart. During her year long engagement, Sarah's fiancé started attending church, was baptized, and was integrated into our family. He had many positive qualities, and we grew to love him. However, my husband and I still could not imagine how Sarah could overlook the lack of maturity, irresponsibility, and lifestyle choices that were so different from her own.

Within a few months of marriage, Sarah realized her mistake, but divorce had never been a part of her plan. As weeks and months went by, Sarah tried to make the best of a miserable situation. She kept up a good front for my husband and me and didn't tell us how the relationship was unraveling. Finally, after eighteen months, Sarah revealed she was moving into another apartment to separate from her husband. Sarah explained she felt she had to leave to save the marriage. She actually hoped that leaving would prompt a change and a new beginning. It didn't. Her husband was ready to regain his freedom and had already resumed his former lifestyle. Sarah offered to join her husband for counseling, but he refused. The unthinkable word, "Divorce," became reality.

Ironically, a similar event was unfolding hundreds of miles away in Morrow, Ohio. Another marriage was ending. A very responsible, mature, Christian man who never imagined himself being divorced was becoming (like Sarah) another divorce statistic. A few years later, Sarah met and married Scott, the man from Ohio. Scott is everything I had hoped and prayed Sarah would find in a husband. I had always envisioned Sarah marrying a man who was a little older than her--a stable Christian man who is strong, and confident enough to earn Sarah's respect yet kind and generous enough to encourage our "take charge" daughter to reach her own potential without being intimidated by her. That's a lot to ask, but God is a mighty God, and Scott is that kind of man. My prayers for Sarah had been delayed, but not denied. Even though life has turned out well for Sarah and Scott, divorce is a terrible disruption to God's plan. Shaking the dust and moving on involves getting past the pain and shame that come with divorce. It means sharing the blame and forgiving oneself as well as the other person. It means learning from the past and not making the same mistake.

APPLICATION: Who is the most difficult person in
your life?

_____

_____

_____

_____

_____

_____

_____

_____

_____

_____

_____

Pray for that person and ask God to give you
spiritual insight, wisdom, and protection. Seek God's
help in leading you to take specific actions while
standing strong in doing what is right but not being
manipulated or abused by the person.

Chapter VI: Flee From Destruction

Pause and Ponder:

A proverb claims, "It is better to live in a corner of the roof than share a house with a quarrelsome wife" (Proverbs 21:9). Consider this principle (not only for a wife) but for anyone who is quarrelsome or destructive.

Word Power:

"Do not repay anyone evil for evil. Be careful to do what is right in the eyes of everybody. If it is possible, as far as it depends on you, live at peace with everyone. Do not take revenge, my friends, but leave room for God's wrath, for it is written: 'It is mine to avenge'..." (Romans 12:17).

Body Builders for Reflection and Discussion:

1. Why is it important to honor positions of authority (government officials, employers, parents, teachers, leaders)?

2. Even though David's kindness resulted in Saul's words of repentance, why do you think David did not return with Saul?

3. Why do you think Saul may have repented at that moment?

4. What are some acceptable ways of dealing with a person who is destructive or irrational?

5. How does honoring a person's position (even though he /she does not deserve it) help *you* shake the dust and move on?

6. How does forgiving oneself and others free you to ***shake the dust and move on***?

VII

Conclusion

There is something powerfully capsulated in the simple phrase: "Shake the dust and move on." It is a positive, energizing command. It's like the first notes of reveille to arise from sleep and move forward. It's like the charge, "Start your engines!" to leave the starting line and begin the race.

The admonition to *shake the dust and move on* addresses both the past and the future. It is a reminder to leave the dirt behind. It is an imperative to remove the dust of bitterness, hurt, resentment, guilt, rejection, anger, worry or anything that emotionally cripples. Facing an unpleasant issue is valuable. Learning from it is wise, but dwelling on it can be harmful. *Shake the dust* is a figurative expression for a very real action to forgive and let go of past grievances and negative emotions.

Lot's wife (Genesis 19:26) is a classic example of a person who looks back. She looks back at the wickedness of Sodom and Gomorrah, the home she has left--even though God commanded that those leaving the evil cities not look back. The backward glance caused Lot's wife to be turned into a pillar of salt. That seems like a rather "stiff" consequence. However, looking back can be just that harmful. A negative situation can sometimes snowball in our emotions and become bigger and bigger each time we allow the revolving door of memory to take us through the emotional journey of the past event.

Dwelling on a past hurt allows bitterness to take root and can lead to discouragement, depression, and a host of unhealthy, negative emotions that can even lead to unpleasant words and negative actions.

Shake the dust is a figurative reminder for a person to separate from the negative baggage of the past before moving on. Distance does not necessarily remove a person from a problem if he takes the hurtful memories and negative emotions with him.

Our first U.S. President, George Washington, offers valuable advice: "We ought not to look back unless it is to derive useful lessons from the past errors, and for the purpose of profiting by dear bought experience."

Shaking the dust is not easy. The more layers of dust that accumulate, the more difficult it is to shake. Unlike sand that rolls off, dust is somewhat adhesive. It sticks to shoes, clothing, and even skin. Sometimes shaking the dust requires more than just a moderate tap to the tip of the shoe. When shoes are really dusty, it may take pounding them on a concrete step or briskly brushing to loosen the dust before it can be removed by shaking. Dust, like the negative emotions of life doesn't just go away on its own. It accumulates until some type of action is taken to get rid of it.

One of the best dust-busters for life's negative circumstances is forgiveness. Like a soothing furniture polish that attracts dust and cleanses an object, forgiveness removes the grit and grime of situations that can abrasively scar our lives. Forgiveness removes life's vacuum cleaner bag filled with dirt. Forgiveness sets a person free to move on.

Moving on, much like shaking the dust, also poses a challenge. How does a person know if it is time or right to move on? Deliberately ending a job, moving away from a situation, or distancing ourselves from a person is not always necessary. However, there are some commonsense guidelines that help determine when moving on is the best choice.

It is best to shake the dust and move on when a situation or circumstance is *unalterable*. When there is absolutely nothing that can be done to change a situation, a person might as well make the best of it by rising above it, moving beyond it, and trusting God for the rest.

It is best to shake the dust and move on when a situation, organization, person, or group is repeatedly

- Destructive or abusive physically, verbally, emotionally, or spiritually.
- Deceitful, devious, or untruthful and shows no remorse, repentance, or commitment to change.

Much can be learned from adversity. People often become kinder, wiser, stronger, more humble individuals through the tough situations they encounter. The most trying circumstances of life often deepen people's faith causing them to trust more in God and less in themselves.

Shaking the dust and moving on, doesn't mean giving up or excusing unacceptable behavior, but it does mean letting go. It means taking the positive memories and valuable lessons learned, while leaving behind the destructive elements of hurt, guilt, pain, sorrow and blame.   It means surrendering the worst in life and embracing God's best.

APPLICATION: What is keeping you from shaking the dust and moving on?

_____

_____

_____

_____

Move closer to God: "Come near to God and he will come near to you" (James 4:8).

1. Acknowledge that sin separates all people from God. "…for all have sinned and fall short of the glory of God" (Rom. 3:23).

2. Confess your sins: "If we claim to be without sin, we deceive ourselves and the truth is not in us. If we confess our sins, he is faithful and just and will forgive us our sins and purify us from all unrighteousness" (I John 1:8-9)

3. Receive God's gift of forgiveness: "For God so loved the world that he gave his one and only Son, that whoever believes in him shall not perish but have eternal life" (John 3:16).

4. Thank God for His forgiveness. Ask Him to help you be more forgiving as you continue to move on with Him.

Chapter VII: Conclusion

Pause and Ponder:

Baptism is an outward symbol of an inward change in a person's life. How can the physical act of baptism, help a person shake the dust and move on?

Word Power:

"Enter through the narrow gate. For wide is the gate and broad is the road that leads to destruction, and many enter through it. But small is the gate and narrow the road that leads to life, and only a few find it" (Matthew 7:13-14).

Body Builders for Reflection and Discussion:

1. How does our own forgiveness in Christ, make it easier for us to forgive others?

2. In what way is forgiveness a cornerstone of health and wholeness?

3. How is reading the Bible and hearing God's word important to growing and becoming rooted in Christ? How does it help to dismantle negative, destructive emotions?

4. Consider God's amazing grace. "For it is by grace you have been saved, through faith—and

this not from yourselves, it is the gift of God—not by works, so that no one can boast. For we are God's workmanship, created in Christ Jesus to do good works, which God prepared in advance for us to do" (Ephesians 2:8-10).

5. Why is finding and spending time with friends who are in Christ helpful in severing the past and moving on with God?

Blessed are those who shake the dust of the world and move on to abundant life in Christ

Works Cited

"All About Dr. Seuss." *Dr. Seuss National Memorial.*
August 1, 2007.
<www.catinthehat.org/history.htm>

Jordan, Michael. "Sports." *BrainyQuote.* August 2, 2007.
<www.brainyquote.com>

Miller, Dan. " 'Inspirational' Speaker." August 2, 2007.
<danmillerspeaker.com>

"Walt Disney: A Short Biography." *JustDisney.Com.*
August 2, 2007.
<www.justdisney.com/walt+disney/biography/
w_bio_short.html>

West, Latoya. "Sylvester Stallone Biography." *About.
com: Reality TV.* August 2, 2007.
http://realitytv.about.com/od/thecontender/a/
SlyStallone_2.htm

All biblical quotes are taken from
The New International Version.

About the Author

Marcia Shepherd is a career educator with more than twenty years experience teaching developmental and college credit composition. Her teaching career followed her husband's former military assignments and provided opportunities to work for three universities and two community colleges. She also worked as an English teacher, counselor, and elementary principal during her thirteen years at Hampton Christian Schools. Marcia has served as a staff writer for both a military and a civilian newspaper. In addition, Marcia has published articles in Officer's Christian Fellowship, *Command*. While working as a stay at home mom with three children, Marcia wrote a weekly newspaper column, "Counselor's Viewpoint," published in *The Mountain View Standard* and *The Thayer Gazette*. Marcia is currently employed as the senior instructional assistant in the Thomas Nelson Community College Writing Center, Hampton, VA.

In addition to her passion for writing, Marcia loves to travel and spend time with her family. Marcia also enjoys being a part of the creative atmosphere and dynamic spiritual growth at Waters Edge Church, Yorktown, VA.

Credentials include:

B.S. in English Education, Truman University, Kirksville, Missouri;

M.S. in Counseling, Missouri State University, Springfield, Missouri,

Postgraduate work in English Education, Century University, Albuquerque, NM

Postgraduate Professional License in English, speech, and counseling from the Commonwealth of VA

Printed in the United States
146219LV00001B/5/A